David
and
Goliath

*written and illustrated
by Duane Porter*

ISBN 978-1-962937-10-8

Illustrations and cover by Duane Porter

Published by
Buried Treasure Publishing
Zephyrhills, Florida

BuriedTreasurePublishing.com

Printed in the U.S.A.

The story of David and Goliath is well-known to nearly everyone. But I've discovered that many have not actually read the story as recorded in the Bible.

That is the story we will share here, with beautiful pictures to illustrate each scene.

Each story has meaning and purpose, to teach about the love of God for us as we remain faithful to Him.

David lived in Israel long ago.

He tended the sheep for his father, Jesse.

David was brave and strong.

When a lion attacked the sheep,
he fought the lion and killed it.

He also slew a bear.

One day David's father asked him to take gifts to his three eldest brothers, who were away fighting the Philistines in a war.

David hurried to obey his father.

When David arrived at the battlefield, the Philistines were assembled on a nearby mountain with a valley between the armies.

A giant warrior, named Goliath of Gath, walked toward the Israelites and issued a challenge.

He called for Israel to send out a challenger to fight him, and whoever won the fight would win the battle between the armies.

Goliath stood over eight feet tall.

His iron spear head weighed
sixteen pounds, and his mail
armor weighed 125 pounds.

He wore a brass helmet, and
brass greaves to protect his shins.
A magnificent sword hung
at his belt.

Goliath even had a man to carry
his great shield before him so the
giant could use both arms
for fighting.

The Philistine giant had repeated his boast for forty days, cursing and insulting the army of Israel and their God.

Saul, the king of Israel, was afraid of Goliath, even though Saul stood a head above the average man and was a great warrior himself.

David was angry when he heard
Goliath's words and curses,
and asked "Who is this Philistine,
that he should defy the armies
of the living God?"

The soldiers were amazed at
David's courage, and told
King Saul that a brave lad was
unafraid to face Goliath.

Saul sent for David to
come to him.

Saul told David, "You cannot fight this giant, for you are but a youth, and he has been a man of war from his youth."

David replied, "I kept my father's sheep, and there came a lion, and a bear, and took a lamb out of the flock. And I went after them, and smote them, and killed them."

"The Lord that delivered me out of the paw of the lion, and out of the paw of the bear, he will deliver me out of the hand of this Philistine."

Saul gave his own armor
to David, but the armor was
too big because Saul was
such a large man.

"I can't wear this," David said,
so he took it off.

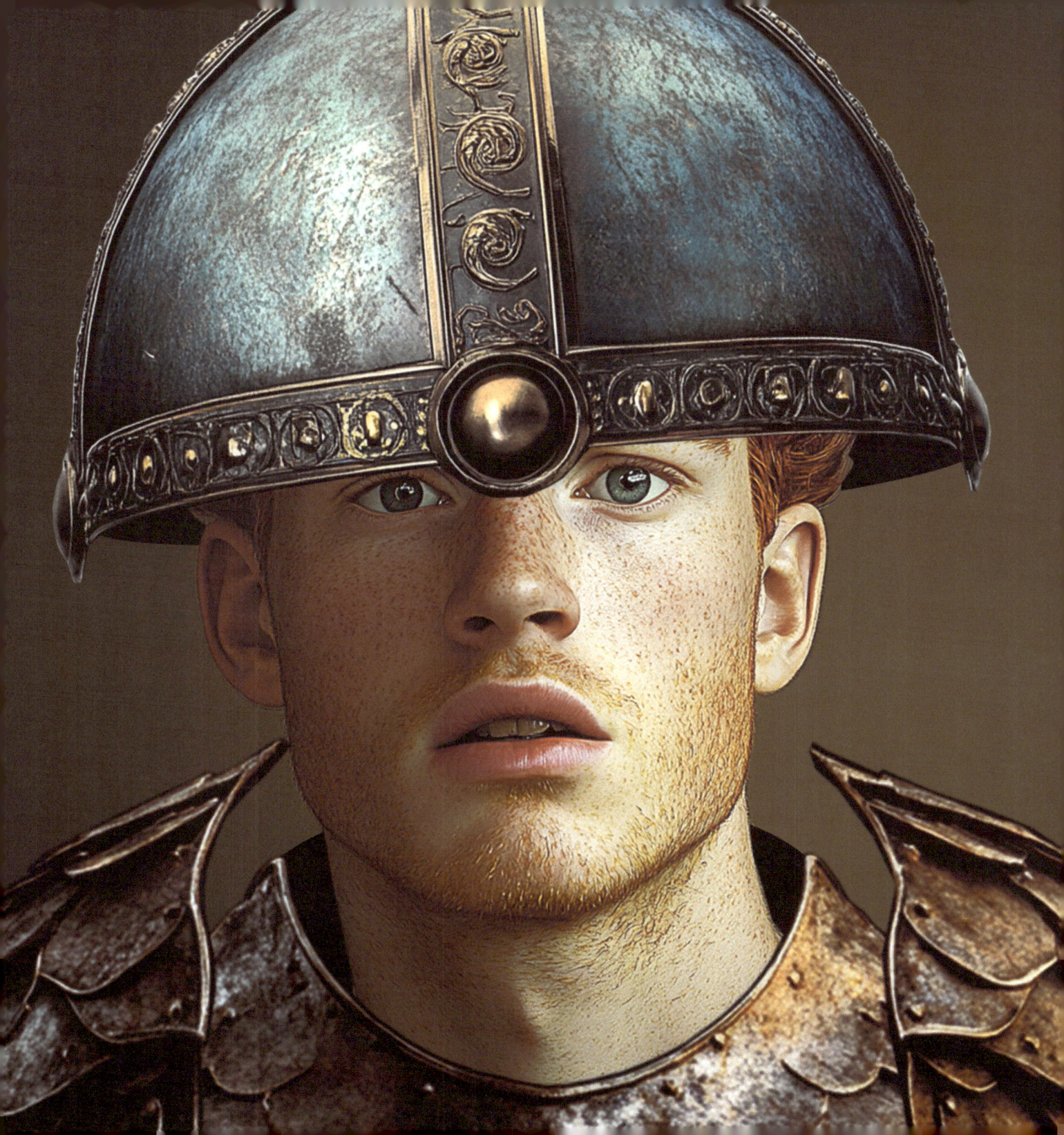

David took his staff,
and chose five smooth stones
out of the brook and put them
in a shepherd's bag he carried.

He picked up his sling
and walked toward Goliath.

Goliath was enraged and offended when he saw David.

"Am I a dog, that you come at me with sticks?" he roared. He cursed David by his Philistine gods.

"Come to me, and I will give your flesh to the fowls of the air, and to the beasts of the field."

David was not afraid. He said,

"You come to me with a sword, and a spear, and a shield, but I come to you in the name of the Lord of hosts, the God of the armies of Israel, who you have defied."

"This day will the Lord deliver you into my hand, and I will smite you, and take your head from you, and I will give the carcasses of the Philistine army to the fowls of the air, and to the wild beasts of the earth, that all the earth may know that there is a God in Israel."

Goliath strode toward David,
but David ran towards Goliath,
swinging his sling and threw a
stone that hit the Philistine
in his forehead.

The giant fell on his face
to the ground.

David ran and took
Goliath's sword
out of its sheath,
and cut
Goliath's head off.

When the Philistines
saw that their champion
was dead, they ran away
and the Israelite army
chased after them.

Now David was a hero. His bravery and faith in God caused the people to love him. Eventually David would become the next king in Israel.